Perspectives

Setting Goals
What's Important?

Series Consultant: Linda Hoyt

Flying Start
to Literacy®

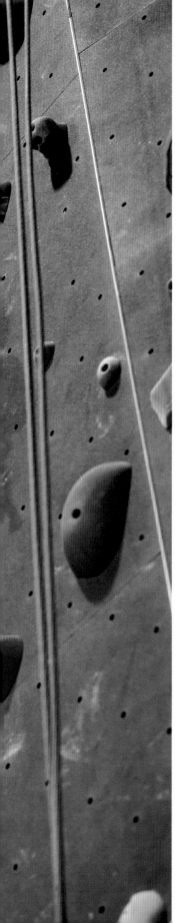

Contents

Introduction

What do you need to think about when setting goals?

"You can do it!"   "Keep on trying!"   "Do your best!"

Many people set goals.   Sometimes, they meet these goals, and sometimes, they don't.   Sometimes, people set goals that are just not realistic.

So what about you?   Do you set goals?   Do you reach your goals?   What inspires you to keep trying?

The tortoise and the hare

This popular story is about two animals that have a race.

Think about the goals of each animal. Why do you think that one animal achieved its goal and the other didn't?

There once was a speedy hare that bragged about how fast he could run.

Tired of hearing him boast, Tortoise challenged Hare to a race. All the animals in the forest gathered to watch.

Hare ran down the road for a while and then paused to rest. He looked back at Tortoise and cried out, "How do you expect to win this race when you are walking along at your slow, slow pace?"

Hare stretched himself out alongside the road and fell asleep, thinking there was plenty of time to relax.

Tortoise walked and walked. He never gave up. He never, ever stopped until he reached the finish line.

The animals that were watching cheered so loudly for Tortoise, they woke up Hare.

Hare stretched and yawned and began to run again, but it was too late. Tortoise was over the line.

After that, Hare always reminded himself:
"Don't brag about your lightning pace, for slow and steady wins the race!"

The light globe

Thomas Edison created the first light globe that could be used to light houses and cities in 1879. Before then, he made 1,000 unsuccessful attempts at inventing the light globe.

What does this make you think?

A reporter asked Edison: "How did it feel to fail 1,000 times?"

Edison replied: "I didn't fail 1,000 times. The light globe was an invention with 1,000 steps."

Speak out!

Read what these students think about setting goals.

Goals help motivate people to keep working and not to give up. Your goal can be anything, but it is important to keep it realistic. If you can't dance, a goal like being a professional dancer is an unrealistic goal and not within reach.

You have to know what you are capable of. If you have a goal and you know you can't reach it now, then you make little goals along the way to help you achieve it.

Goal setting is good because it sets a target that you believe you can achieve. However, circumstances may change, and it may be that you have to give up or change your goal.

Reaching a goal can be hard work. If you set a goal, it has to be worth it because you have to work hard to achieve it.

So it's important to set goals that are worth the time and effort you have to put in to achieve them.

Is it okay to quit?

Written by Kerrie Shanahan

Not everyone can reach the goals they set themselves.

So, is it okay to quit? Eight-year-old James thinks it is. Do you agree with him?

When I was seven, I started two new after-school
activities – piano and soccer.

I was really nervous before my first piano lesson.
I knew nothing about piano, and I didn't know the
other two kids in the class.   But it was fine.

My teacher Izzy was very positive, and she smiled a lot, even
when I played the wrong notes.   I loved practising the new
skills Izzy taught me, and I couldn't wait for each lesson.

I was excited to start playing soccer. Three boys from my class were joining, too, so I wasn't nervous at all.

But, to my surprise, I didn't enjoy it. We did lots of drills, and we had to repeat them if we didn't do them right. We did one drill after another, and we had no time for fun.

The boys from my class were really good, and they loved it. This made me feel even more left out.

I started dreading soccer.

After a while, Mum noticed and asked me what was wrong. I told her, we talked about it, and she said I didn't have to go to soccer anymore. I was so relieved.

I still love playing the piano. My new friends and I even play in concerts. I have also started playing tennis, and I really enjoy it!

My advice is to give things a try, but if you really don't like it, it's okay to quit.

How to write about your opinion

State your opinion

Think about the main question in the introduction on page 4 of this book. What is your opinion?

Research

Look for other information that you need to back up your opinion.

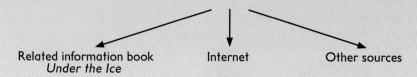

| Related information book *Under the Ice* | Internet | Other sources |

Make a plan

Introduction

How will you "hook" the reader to get them interested?

Write a sentence that makes your opinion clear.

List reasons to support your opinion.

Support your reason with examples.   Support your reason with examples.   Support your reason with examples.

Conclusion

Write a sentence that makes your opinion clear. Leave your reader with a strong message.

Publish

Publish your writing.

Include some graphics or visual images.

16